Protecting the EARTH'S ANIMALS

Animal Testing
Attacking a Controversial Problem

BOB WOODS

PROTECTING *the* **EARTH'S ANIMALS**

Animal Testing

Attacking a Controversial Problem

BY BOB WOODS

Mason Crest
450 Parkway Drive, Suite D
Broomall, PA 19008
www.masoncrest.com

© 2018 by Mason Crest, an imprint of National Highlights, Inc.

Printed and bound in the United States of America.

Series ISBN: 978-1-4222-3872-1
Hardback ISBN: 978-1-4222-3873-8
EBook ISBN: 978-1-4222-7910-6

First printing
1 3 5 7 9 8 6 4 2

Produced by Shoreline Publishing Group LLC
Santa Barbara, California
Editorial Director: James Buckley Jr.
Designer: Patty Kelley
www.shorelinepublishing.com

Library of Congress Cataloging-in-Publication Data
Names: Woods, Bob.
Title: Animal testing : attacking a controversial problem / By Bob Woods.
Description: Broomall, PA : Mason Crest, [2018] |
Series: Protecting the Earth's animals | Includes index.
Identifiers: LCCN 2017003635| ISBN 9781422238738 (hardback) | ISBN 9781422238721 (series) |
    ISBN 9781422279106 (ebook)
Subjects: LCSH: Animal experimentation–Juvenile literature.
Classification: LCC HV4915 .W657 2018 | DDC 179/.4–dc23 LC record available at https://lccn.loc.
    gov/2017003635

Cover photographs by Dreamstime.com: Verastuchelova (top); Shutterstock: Niderlander (bottom)

QR Codes disclaimer:

CONTENTS

KEY ICONS TO LOOK FOR

Words to Understand: These words with their easy-to-understand definitions will increase the reader's understanding of the text, while building vocabulary skills.

Sidebars: This boxed material within the main text allows readers to build knowledge, gain insights, explore possibilities, and broaden their perspectives by weaving together additional information to provide realistic and holistic perspectives.

Educational Videos: Readers can view videos by scanning our QR codes, providing them with additional educational content to supplement the text. Examples include news coverage, moments in history, speeches, iconic moments, and much more!

Text-Dependent Questions: These questions send the reader back to the text for more careful attention to the evidence presented here.

Research Projects: Readers are pointed toward areas of further inquiry connected to each chapter. Suggestions are provided for projects that encourage deeper research and analysis.

Series Glossary of Key Terms: This back-of-the-book glossary contains terminology used throughout this series. Words found here increase the reader's ability to read and comprehend higher-level books and articles in this field.

WORDS TO UNDERSTAND

biopsies   surgical procedures intended to test a body part for disease, usually cancer

contentious   heavily debated, loudly disputed

humane   showing compassion or care

preserve   an area of land set aside for a specific purpose

primates   a group of mammals that include apes, monkeys, and humans; they have the use of their hands and have high levels of social interaction

Welcome to Chimp Haven. This is a beautiful, 200-acre **preserve** in western Louisiana filled with pine forests, natural grasslands, and freshwater ponds. Officially named the National Chimpanzee Sanctuary, Chimp Haven was established by the U.S. government in 1995. Today it's home to Penny, Violet, Julius, Ned, and nearly 200 other chimps.

These aren't just any chimpanzees, though. Most of them are elderly **primates** who have been sent here from research laboratories around the country. For years—in some cases decades—they were subjects in medical and scientific research, tests, and experiments. The tests were designed to learn more about human behavior and diseases such as cancer, hepatitis, and HIV/AIDS. Because chimpanzees are so genetically similar to humans, researchers believe that studying them can lead to new treatments and cures. While Penny, Ned, and the other residents at Chimp Haven have "retired," there still are hundreds of chimps being used for research.

The tests are often painful and distressing, according to the **Humane** Society of the United States (HSUS), part of a worldwide organization that protects the rights of all animals. The procedures include liver **biopsies**, human virus infections, and "knockdowns," in which a chimpanzee is shot with a tranquilizer gun. The chimps live alone in closet-size metal cages. "This type of confinement and isolation," the Humane Society reports, "can cause severe problems in chimpanzees, such as depression, heightened aggression, frustration, and even self-mutilation."

The HSUS is among many groups and individuals working to completely eliminate or greatly decrease all types of animal testing. They consider such testing to be cruel, painful, immoral, and unethical. Besides chimpanzees and other nonhuman primates, animals used in tests include dogs, cats, rabbits, pigs, horses, sheep, goats, mice, rats, birds, and frogs.

While comprehensive statistics are not available, several animal rights groups estimate that more than 25 million vertebrate animals (those with a skeleton made of bone) are used in research, testing, and education in the U.S. every year. The organization People for the Ethical Treatment of Animals (PETA) claims that more than 100 million ani-

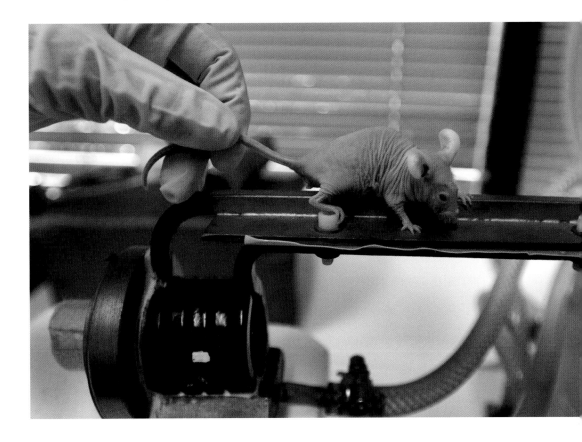

This mouse with a tumor is being used in research on how magnets can be used to treat cancer.

Protesters marched against animal use by a school in Canada.

mals die in the U.S. every year in various types of research and experiments.

Opponents to animal testing argue that animals suffer physically and mentally—and can die—when used in experiments to test medical procedures and devices, drugs, cosmetics, and chemicals. They further claim that many animals have rights to live free from cruelty and suffering. Besides, opponents contend, there are effective, high-tech alternatives for such testing. Such options include 3-D computer simulations, life-like mannequins, and artificial tissue and organs. Plus, they say, animals are very different from human beings and therefore make poor test subjects. For example, drugs that pass animal tests are not necessarily safe for humans.

On the other hand, those who conduct and support animal testing insist that the animals are treated humanely. Researchers say that they follow federal rules established by Congress in the Animal Welfare Act (AWA), first signed into law in 1966, as well as state and local regulations.

Research supporters point to the many medical procedures, drugs, and products, first tested on animals, that have cured human diseases and saved lives. The California Biomedical Research Association states that nearly every medical breakthrough in the last 100 years has resulted directly from research using animals. Examples include the discovery of insulin to treat diabetes and vaccines to prevent polio and hepatitis B.

The public and frequently **contentious** debate over animal testing has persisted for more than a century, not only in the U.S., but in many other countries. Laws have been passed to abolish certain types of animal research and to protect research animals from inhumane treatment. Scientists have successfully adopted alternative methods that don't involve animals. Nonetheless, millions of animals are still subjected to testing, and so the controversy continues.

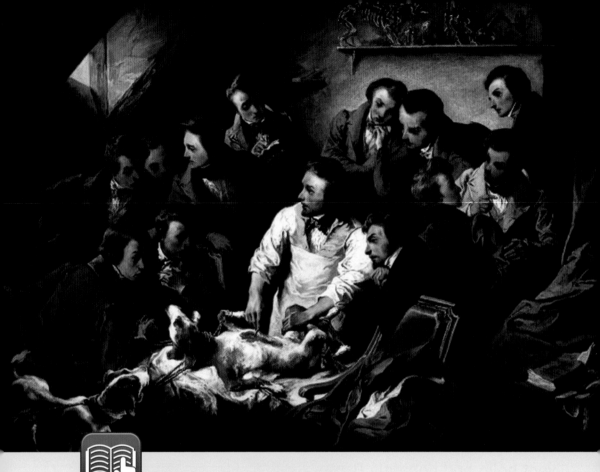

WORDS TO UNDERSTAND

dissection   the surgical cutting of a dead animal

euthanized   killed with chemicals to end or ease suffering

Freedom of Information Act   a federal law that forces US government agencies to turn over documents and information when requested by the press or the public

mandated   called for by law or regulation

pesticides   chemicals used to kill bothersome or dangerous insects

vivisection   the surgical cutting of a live animal for experimental purposes

HISTORY OF ANIMAL TESTING

The first known experiments by humans on animals were in ancient Greece. The philosopher and scientist Aristotle, who lived from 382 to 322 BCE, wrote about performing tests on live animals as a way to understand how the human body functions. Erasistratus (304–250 BCE) was a physician who founded a school of anatomy in Alexandria, Greece. Based on his **dissections** of animals, he identified the valves of the heart and the difference between the veins and arteries that circulate blood to and from that vital organ.

Fast forward to ancient Rome, where philosopher and physician Galen (130–200) dissected pigs, goats, and even an elephant during his studies of human anatomy. He has been referred to as the "father of **vivisection**."

It wasn't until the 12th century that surgery was conducted on humans. Avenzoar (1094–1162), a well-known physician in medieval Spain, dissected animals as a way of testing surgical procedures before performing them on human patients.

During the 1800s, animal testing led to several important medical discoveries. French chemist and microbiologist Louis Pasteur (1822–1895) is best known for developing pasteurization—the process of heating liquids, such as milk, to destroy harmful bacteria—in 1864. But for several years before then, he studied the relationship between germs and disease by injecting sheep with anthrax, a germ that can kill humans and animals.

Dogs were operated on to isolate and test insulin as a treatment for diabetes, most notably by Canadian physician

Pasteur's ideas helped make food safer.

PAVLOV'S DOGS

Russian physiologist Ivan Pavlov (1849–1936) performed experiments on dogs to prove that certain animal behaviors can be learned. He famously trained dogs to salivate every time they heard the sound of an electric buzzer. Pavlov subjected each dog to a minor operation, running a tube from their internal saliva ducts to a small glass funnel affixed to the outside of their mouths so that he could observe the animals salivating.

Frederick Banting (1891–1941) in 1921. Banting and fellow researcher J. J. R. Macleod were jointly awarded the 1923 Nobel Prize for Physiology or Medicine.

In the 1940s, experiments on guinea pigs spurred development of antibiotics that cured tuberculosis, and monkeys were used in the discovery of the vaccine to cure polio. Research on rodents, rabbits, dogs, cats, and monkeys during the 1950s led to new anesthetics given to human patients during surgery. Since the 1960s, animal experiments conducted at pharmaceutical companies, universities, medical schools, hospitals, and government and private research labs have pioneered human organ transplants and antirejection medications. They have also advanced antibiotics and vaccines, and drugs to treat HIV/AIDS, Alzheimer's disease, multiple sclerosis, and spinal cord injuries.

Animals in Space

When the United States began its space exploration program in the late 1940s, dogs, monkeys, chimpanzees, and other animals were strapped inside rockets and launched into outer space for various types of biomedical tests. For example, before sending the first humans into gravity-free space, scientists wanted to find out how astronauts might be affected by weightlessness, especially over long periods of time. From 1948 to 1950, U.S. researchers sent several rhesus monkeys into space. Although the rockets blasted off successfully, the monkeys onboard died during reentry.

The first monkey to survive a space flight was a rhesus named Yorick. On September 20, 1951, Yorick and 11 mice rode inside the nose cone of an Aerobee missile sent high above Holloman Air Force Base in New Mexico, and they all landed alive.

Nearly six months later, two Philippine monkeys, Patricia and Mike, took off from Holloman aboard an Aerobee rocket. The experiment is described in a NASA report, *A Brief History of Animals in Space*: "Patricia was placed in a seated position and Mike in a prone [flat] position to determine differences in the effects of rapid acceleration. Fired 36 miles [58 km] up at a speed of 2,000 mph [3218 kph], these two monkeys were the first primates to reach such a high altitude." The nose cone containing the monkeys, plus two white mice being tested for weightlessness, was safely recovered with all four animals alive.

A monkey named Ham was part of an early US space flight.

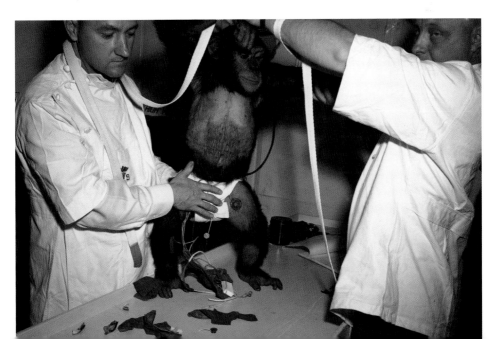

Meanwhile, the Soviet Union was developing its space program, competing with the U.S. in what became known as the "space race." During the early 1950s, a series of Soviet rockets carried dogs into Earth's upper atmosphere. Some survived, several did not.

On October 4, 1957, the Soviets launched *Sputnik 1*, a spherical satellite about the size of a beach ball. It made history as the first spacecraft to successfully orbit Earth. A month later, *Sputnik 2* blasted off from the U.S.S.R.'s Baikonur Cosmodrome with a dog aboard. Laika was a stray mixed-breed—in other words, a mutt—reportedly picked up on the streets of Moscow and trained for space flight. She became an international celebrity as the first living creature to orbit our planet.

The website SpaceToday.org describes Laika's momentous—and ultimately harrowing—journey: "Laika was supported inside the satellite by a harness that allowed some movement and access to food and water. Electrodes transmitted vital signs including heartbeat, blood pressure, and breathing rate. The American press nicknamed the dog Muttnik. She captured the hearts of people around the world as the batteries that operated her life-support system ran down and the capsule air ran out. Life slipped away from

Laika a few days into her journey. Later, *Sputnik 2* fell into the atmosphere and burned on April 14, 1958."

Throughout the next five decades, both the U.S. and U.S.S.R. continued to send monkeys, dogs, and other nonhuman species into space aboard a variety of spacecraft, including the Apollo rockets, the International Space Station, and the Space

A lizard native to South America spent time on the Space Station.

Shuttle. The record for most animals in space was set on April 17, 1998, when more than 2,000 creatures—among them rats, mice, fish, crickets, and snails—joined the seven-member crew of the shuttle *Columbia* for a 16-day mission.

Although the flights resulted in many animals dying, NASA sums up its research on a positive note: "Over the past fifty years, American and Soviet scientists have utilized the animal world for testing. Despite losses, these animals have taught the scientists a tremendous amount more than could have been learned without them. Without animal testing in the early days of the human space program, the Soviet and American programs could have suffered great losses of human life. These animals performed a service to their respective countries that no human could or would have performed. They gave their lives and/or their service in the name of technological advancement, paving the way for humanity's many forays into space."

The U.S. Department of Defense has experimented on millions of live animals for decades. Monkeys have been exposed to deadly diseases, chemicals, and radiation to test how soldiers might react to them on the battlefield. Military researchers also subject animals to extreme heat and cold, lack of oxygen, sleeplessness, isolation, and other physical and mental stressors to study their effects on troops. In training military emergency medical personnel to treat wounds and injuries to humans,

Monkeys have been used to help members of the military.

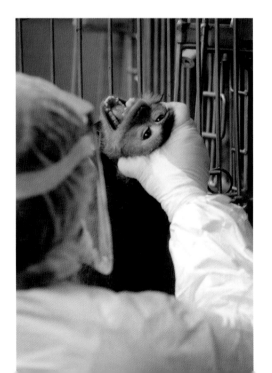

goats and pigs are made victim to gunshots, bomb blasts, stabbings, burns, amputations, and bone breaks. Although the animals are usually given an anesthesia beforehand, if they survive the trauma and treatment, they're **euthanized** afterward.

Education and Medicine

High schools, universities, and veterinary and medical schools in the U.S. exploit an estimated 20 million animals for education and testing every year, according to PETA, about half of which are killed for classroom dissection. Until recently, medical and veterinary school students performed so-called "non-survival surgeries" on live animals—including dogs, cats, pigs, and goats—in which the animals were euthanized before they awoke from anesthesia. While U.S. medical schools have used alternative training methods, some veterinary schools continue the practice.

The U.S. Food and Drug Administration (FDA) oversees the safety of foods, drugs, cosmetics, and medical devices. Since Congress passed the Federal Food, Drug, and Cosmetic Act in 1938, the agency has required companies making such products to test them, including all the ingredients used, before they're sold to the public. Animal testing is not **mandated** by the FDA, yet it has been the preferred method for decades. Non-animal alternatives, proven to be equally effective, have become available and adopted by many companies.

Makers of cosmetics and personal-care products—ranging from mascara and lipstick to toothpaste and shampoo—have a long history of animal testing. While the European Union, India, Australia, and other countries have banned animal testing for cosmetics, the U.S. has not.

There are several common cosmetics tests performed on rabbits, mice, rats, and guinea pigs. One involves rubbing chemicals onto the animals' shaved skin or dripping them into their eyes. Another force-feeds substances for weeks or months to see if the animals develop cancers, birth defects, or other abnormalities. There are also so-called "lethal-dose" tests, in which animals ingest large amounts of a substance to determine what dosage results in death. Despite experiencing pain and suffering during the tests, the animals usually don't receive any pain relief, and survivors are routinely killed afterward.

The U.S. Environmental Protection Agency (EPA) is the only federal agency that officially requires animal testing, but only to determine whether **pesticides** are harmful to humans and wildlife. According to the HSUS, nearly 500 products are tested by pesticide makers each year, resulting in thousands of rabbits, rats, mice, and guinea pigs suffering and dying. Other testing methods have been developed, and in 2016 the EPA announced a plan to significantly reduce the use of animal testing.

Fast-breeding white rats are popular in labs.

The U.S. Department of Agriculture (USDA) oversees an animal testing program at its U.S. Meat Animal Research Center in Clay Center, Nebraska. In operation since 1965 and funded by taxpayer dollars, the center conducts research on cows, pigs, and sheep. The USDA says that tests are to improve food safety and help make the American meat industry more efficient and competitive globally. However, a 2015 report by the *The New York Times* documented abuse of the center's farm animals, "which have been subjected to illness, pain, and premature death over many years," the article stated.

Based on interviews with current and former employees at the center, as well as internal documents obtained through the **Freedom of Information Act**, the *Times* cited pig-breeding experiments that produced larger litters of piglets. As a tragic outcome, though, "hundreds of those newborns, too frail or crowded to move, are being crushed each year when their mothers roll over." Cows were bred to give birth to more calves, "which often emerge weakened or deformed, dying in such numbers that even meat producers have been repulsed." And in an effort to develop "easy care"

sheep—meaning without indoor shelters or human handlers—"ewes are giving birth, unaided, in open fields where newborns are killed by predators, harsh weather, and starvation."

Officials at the center and the USDA defended the testing program and treatment of the thousands of animals in it. Nonetheless, animal rights advocates demanded reforms, especial-

Piglets like these crowd in pens, but critics say one facility went too far.

ly because the Animal Welfare Act, which aims to minimize suffering mostly of dogs and cats used in testing, doesn't cover farm animals. Shortly after the article was published, a bill was introduced in Congress to amend the AWA to include farm animals. As of this writing, the bill is still being considered.

New York Times report on USMRAC

 TEXT-DEPENDENT QUESTIONS

1. Name three types of animals that have been to space.

2. What do veterinary students do that is a controversial use of animals?

3. Why does the EPA still use animal testing?

 RESEARCH PROJECT

Pick your favorite personal care product or makeup. Research how the company that makes it performs tests on its safety. Do they use animals? What other methods do they use?

THE DEBATE OVER ANIMAL TESTING

The issue of animal testing has been debated for centuries. Discussions have been about the science, morality, and ethics of the research and experiments, as well as the treatment of the animals subjected to them. Those in favor include government, academic, and private researchers and food, drug, and cosmetics manufacturers. Those people say that what is learned from animal testing leads to better and safer medical care, food, and various consumer products for humans. That's partly because animals' biological systems are closely related to those of humans. People who support testing also say that humans have the moral authority to use animals for their benefit, often citing religious references. They also claim that the animals are humanely cared for before, during, and after testing, in accordance with the Animal Welfare Act and other regulations.

Opponents of animal testing agree on the importance of providing people with safe healthcare and food. However, they argue that effective alternative testing methods exist. They maintain that animals have the right to be treated humanely in general, and that intentionally causing pain and suffering is cruel, regardless of the species. What's more, critics say, results of tests on animals don't always translate to humans.

Opposing Groups

As far back as the mid 1600s, antivivisectionists—people against surgery on live animals—in Europe **decried** that practice for anatomy studies. Over the next two centuries, the antivivisection movement grew alongside the **domestication** of dogs and cats as household pets. In 1875, the Society for the Protection of Animals Liable to Vivisection was founded in England. A year later, the British Parliament passed the Cruelty to Animals Act, a law regulating animal testing.

The arguments between pro- and anti-animal testing forces continued in England. They boiled over in a famous political controversy known as the "brown dog affair," which raged from 1903 to 1910. It began with protests following the vivisection of a brown terrier in front of a group of medical students at a London university. The researcher sued the protesters for **libel** and won. In 1906, a statue memorializing the dog was erected in a London park, angering pro-animal testing medical students. The statue was repeatedly vandalized, and in 1907, the opposing sides and police officers squared off in a series of riots. The statue was taken down in 1910 and reportedly destroyed. Years

A new "brown dog" statue stands today in a London park.

later, antivivisectionists commissioned a new statue, which replaced the original one in 1985.

The antivivisection movement was gaining momentum in the U.S. by the mid-19th century. In 1866, the American Society for the Prevention of Cruelty to Animals (ASPCA) was founded in New York by Henry Bergh, an American diplomat who had been stationed in Russia. Deeply disturbed

 THE THREE R'S

A similar set of standards that addressed the ethics of animal testing was introduced in 1959 by two British scientists, William Russell and Rex Burch. They suggested that researchers adopt the Three Rs:

• **Replacement:** methods that avoid or replace the use of animals in research.

• **Reduction:** methods that minimize the number of animals used per experiment.

• **Refinement:** methods that minimize suffering and improve animal welfare.

Those guiding principles are used internationally among research scientists and organizations, as well as some animal-rights groups.

by witnessing the beating of a horse there, he returned to the U.S. and resigned his post. He committed himself to combating animal cruelty, from overburdened work-horses to dog fighting.

ASPCA turns 150 years old

By the middle of the 20th century, the use of animals in public and private research in the U.S. continued to expand. Criticism grew as well, but efforts to pass laws protecting animals failed. At the same time, those within the research community defended their practices. For example, the National Society for Medical Research (NSMR) was founded in 1945 by three physicians at the University of Illinois Medical School "to improve public understanding of the principles, methods, and needs of the biological services," the group stated.

While animal-rights laws didn't happen, the NSMR (now the National Association for Biomedical Research) and its allies lobbied in favor of "pound seizure" state laws that were passed during the 1940s and 1950s across the country. These let researchers obtain unclaimed stray dogs and cats from public and private shelters. Some of those laws remain on the books today, though others have been repealed or amended by individual states.

In 1950, five Chicago-area veterinarians organized the Animal Care Panel (ACP, now the American Association for Laboratory Animal Science) to promote animal research and the humane treatment of lab animals. At the time, rules about animal testing and care were inconsistent. In 1963, the ACP published the first edition of *The Guide for the Care and Use of Laboratory Animals*. The *Guide*, as it's known, is still issued periodically by the National Academy of Sciences, a private, non-profit organization of researchers. Its purpose "is to assist institutions in caring for and using animals in ways judged to be scientifically, technically, and humanely appropriate."

New Evidence Changes the Debate

Despite such guidelines and justifications for animal testing, opposition mounted in the 1960s, focusing on the treatment of the animals. A pivotal moment came from an unlikely source: *Sports Illustrated*. In its November 29, 1965, issue, the weekly magazine featured an article entitled "The Lost Pets that Stray to the Labs." In **graphic**, and often disturbing, detail, it told the story of Pepper, a five-year-old Dalmatian that disappeared from the farm of Mr. and Mrs. Peter Lakavage in Slatington, Pennsylvania, in

June of that year. "Nine days later [Pepper] turned up at New York City's Montefiore Hospital, where her body was used in a scientific experiment and then cremated," wrote *SI*'s Coles Phinizy.

The article said that laboratories, which needed dogs and cats for their research, relied on a network of law-abiding dealers to provide them. But it exposed how illegal dognappers around the country were supplying some of those dealers. "Many pet dogs are being stolen from the front lawns and sidewalks of this country," the article stated, "and the thefts in large part are motivated by science's constant and growing need for laboratory animals."

The story not only outraged *SI* readers, but a week later incited New York Congressman Joseph Resnick to introduce a bill that would require anyone dealing in dogs to be licensed by the federal government and to keep records of all transactions. During a hearing on the bill, Resnick noted that it was not intended to deal with animal testing itself

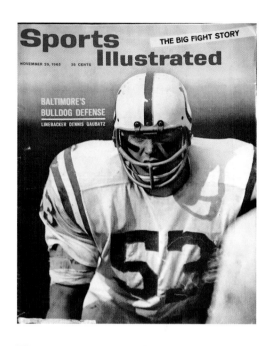

The cover says "football," but a story inside galvanized pet owners.

or the treatment of lab animals, but rather the issue of dognapping. Even so, researchers fought against the legislation, saying that it would interfere with their scientific work and favored the antivivisectionist crusade.

While Resnick's bill and subsequent animal-rights measures were being considered in Congress, public outrage was further fueled by another shocking magazine article, this one in the February 4, 1966, issue of *Life* Magazine. "Concentration Camps for Dogs" described how dognappers were selling pets to dealers, some that were keeping

Sadly, the lessons of the past are not learned. This raid in Texas rescued dogs and other abused animals from a clinic.

"big inventories of dogs in unspeakably filthy compounds. ... Many do not sell directly to labs but simply dispose of their packs at auction where the going rate is 30 cents a pound." Eventually, the article reported, many of those dogs either ended up in the labs—or worse.

The account included horrifying photos taken by *Life*'s Stan Wayman, who accompanied agents of the HSUS and Maryland state troopers on an early-morning raid. The group entered the property of a legal animal dealer outside of Baltimore that housed more than 100 dogs. The article's black-and-white images pictured **emaciated** dogs chained to crude wooden boxes too small to hold them. One photo focused on a large hound that had frozen to death. The authorities rescued the most sickly dogs and charged the dealer with multiple counts of animal cruelty. Yet because there were no laws allowing them to, they couldn't shut down his grisly operation.

A New Law Is Passed

That frustrating situation changed a few months later when President Lyndon Johnson signed the Animal Welfare Act (AWA) into law. It authorized the U.S. Secretary of Agriculture to regulate the transport, sale, and handling of

These crates hold animals saved from a puppy mill.

dogs, cats, nonhuman primates, guinea pigs, hamsters, and rabbits intended to be used in research or "for other purposes." It also required licensing and inspection of dog and cat dealers and humane handling at auction sales.

Animal-rights advocates were quick to point out that the AWA didn't cover rats, mice, fish, and birds—which even today make up around 95 percent of the animals used in research—and lobbied to broaden the law. The first amendment to the AWA came in 1970, expanding coverage to include all warm-blooded animals and including circuses, zoos, shows, and wholesale pet dealers. However, the revision **exempted** retail pet stores, agricultural fairs, rodeos, and dog and cat shows.

Amendments have been made over the years to oversee animal dealers and exhibitors, improve handling and treatment of lab animals, and outlaw dogfighting. A more recent change put rules in place for so-called puppy mills, breeding operations that have a history of inhumane conditions and treatment. To the disappointment of animal-rights advocates, though, the AWA still excludes birds, rats, and mice bred for research, horses not used for research, and other farm animals used in food production. Lobbying efforts and public campaigns to further amend the AWA continue.

 ## TEXT-DEPENDENT QUESTIONS

1. What was the "brown dog" debate in England about?
2. What two magazines helped expose animal cruelty?
3. What are the "3 Rs"?

 ## RESEARCH PROJECT

Just as magazines did the in the 1950s and 1960s, other journalists are doing today. Go online and find recent articles about the exposure of animals misused in some way. Write a short report on the issues of the particular case.

WORDS TO UNDERSTAND

adverse negative, not helpful

physiology the study of human bodies and how they work

REPLACING ANIMAL TESTING

Both sides in the debate over animal testing generally agree that finding alternative methods remains a goal. Some animal-rights advocates insist that the only alternative is an outright ban on using animals in any type of research. Others have adopted the 3Rs—replace, reduce, and refine, an approach favored by researchers. They say that *any* change in animal testing should be considered an alternative, especially when it involves more humane conditions and treatment.

One of the major non-animal alternatives is referred to as *in vitro* testing. That means making human cells, tissues, and organs in a laboratory. Researchers can then expose them to drugs, chemicals, cosmetics ingredients, and other substances to test for **adverse** reactions.

Harvard University's Wyss Institute has developed "organs-on-chips," microchips about the size of a computer flash drive. These devices can mimic human lungs, intestines, kidneys, hearts, brains, and other organs. A lung-on-a-chip is currently being used by the pharmaceutical maker Johnson & Johnson to produce drugs to treat pulmonary thrombosis, a lung disease. The company plans to use a

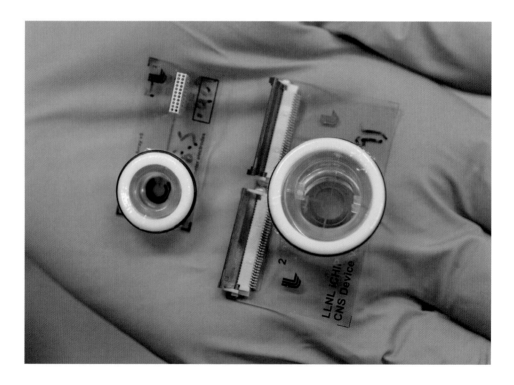

Chips such as these will replace animals for some tests.

liver-on-a-chip to test for poisons in the liver. Wyss also intends to build an entire human-body-on-a-chip—10 different human organs-on-chips linked together to mimic whole-body **physiology**.

Using artificial skin in testing

EpiSkin, EpiDerm, and SkinEthic are lab-produced models of human skin. They can replace the use of rabbits, guinea pigs, and mice in painful experiments in which the animals are injected with a substance or have it applied to their shaved skin to test for allergic responses. While companies that make cosmetics and other personal care and household products still use animals in tests, many are also experimenting with these human-like skins as alternatives.

3-D Modeling and More

Another alternative is the use of sophisticated, 3-D computer models that simulate how the human body functions. They can replace animals in biomedical research and drug tests.

Other complex computer models, known as quantitative structure-activity relationships (QSARs), can replace animal tests by making virtual estimates of a substance's likelihood of being harmful. Major pharmaceutical companies are experimenting with QSARs as a replacement for their ongoing animal testing.

Computer-controlled human mannequins—popularly known as crash-test dummies—are used instead of live animals, including pigs, to test how well cars protect drivers in accidents. Other types of computerized simulators are replacing live animals in tests conducted by the military and in medical schools.

Animal testing for new consumer products is usually

Crash test dummies can be used in place of live subjects.

completed before those products are tested on humans. Another non-animal alternative brings humans into the process earlier. For example, in testing the safety of new drugs, researchers are using a method called microdosing. Human volunteers are given a very small quantity of the drug to test its effects on cells, without affecting the whole body system—and without using non-human animals.

In other microdosing experiments, human volunteers are given advanced brain scans to test the drugs' effects on the central nervous system. This avoids the use of rats, cats, monkeys, and other animals whose brains are damaged in such tests.

Cosmetics: The Ongoing Battle

Throughout the world, the cosmetics industry has been a particular target of animal-rights campaigns due to its history of widespread use of animals in testing products and ingredients. The original reason was to make sure that such products were not harmful to humans. But there are other ways to discover that. The industry has responded by switching to an assortment of alternative methods. Today virtually every major cosmetics and personal care products company—among them Procter & Gamble, L'Oréal,

SAFE SPACES

In the meantime, tests on animals for cosmetics are already banned in many countries, including the European Union, Israel, India, Norway, Turkey, Australia, New Zealand and, most recently, Taiwan.

Unilever, Avon, and Estee Lauder—now features a section on their website explaining their policy on animal testing. The language often mentions that the company does not test its products or ingredients on animals anywhere in the world unless required by law.

That last part, however, "unless required by law," remains controversial. In many countries—including the U.S.—animal testing continues, because some countries require it by law, in particular China. But even that situation is beginning to change. According to PETA, the Chinese Food and Drug Administration has waived its requirement for certain cosmetics to be registered with the agency, which will mean that animal tests for "non-special use" cosmetics will no longer automatically be required.

In June 2015, several members of the U.S. House of Representatives, both Democrats and Republicans, introduced the Humane Cosmetics Act. Under the proposed law, animal testing for cosmetics in the United States would be phased out within one year of enactment and the sale of cosmetics tested on animals would be prohibited within three years. "Subjecting animals to painful and inhumane testing is not who we are as a country," said one of the bill's sponsors, Rep. Martha McSally, a Republican from Arizona. Said her Democratic colleague and fellow sponsor, Don Beyer of Virginia: "Safer, more cost-effective, and completely humane alternatives already exist, and the United States is in no danger of losing its role as a competitive leader in the global cosmetics industry. Now we need to ensure our place as a moral leader." The bill is still being debated in Congress.

Consumers spend hundreds of billions of dollars on cosmetic products every year, and more and more people are demanding that

Look for labels like this one on cosmetics and clothing.

PeTA

Cruelty-Free

This bunny acts as PETA's seal of approval for products.

those products don't involve animal testing. In response, several animal-rights groups have organized "cruelty free" shopping campaigns and guides. PETA maintains a cruelty-free shopping database on its website that identifies companies that do and don't use animal testing. Eight groups, including the HSUS and NEAVS, have banded together to form the Coalition for Consumer Information on Cosmetics, which promotes a single comprehensive standard and an internationally recognized Leaping Bunny logo.

The use of alternative methods to animal testing are growing, but more are needed to help fully end the process.

TEXT–DEPENDENT QUESTIONS

1. What are "organs on chips"?

2. What is microdosing?

3. Why did cosmetics companies test on animals?

 ## RESEARCH PROJECT

Look at some of the household products you or your family use. Do any of them say "animal test free," or similar language? Find examples of three or four companies that use their non-testing status to promote their products.

WORDS TO UNDERSTAND

confiscation   the legal removal of property

vociferous   loud, outspoken, demonstrative

FIGHTING ANIMAL TESTING

From the 1600s until today, opposition to animal testing has evolved into a global network of organizations and individuals. They believe that their efforts need to be more urgent than ever. Today's society demands newer and better healthcare, cosmetics, and other products and procedures that are developed with animal testing.

Animal-rights supporters are educating the general public, researchers, and the business community about the moral and ethical injustice testing can inflict on animals. They also point out the pain and suffering testing causes the innocent subjects. That outcry, combined with increased awareness, has helped lead to alternative methods that achieve the same goals. It has also helped create new laws, regulations, and policies to protect animals from abuse. And although animal testing continues and strong disagreements over its necessity persist, the prospects of ending such inhumane practices are real.

PETA in Action

There are dozens of animal-rights organizations around the world. Some focus on protecting particular species, such as birds, dogs and cats, or gorillas. Some concentrate on reducing animal cruelty in general or promote vegetarianism and veganism. Some are more radical in their efforts than others, organizing covert raids on laboratories to set the animals free. Some operate internationally, others locally. It's safe to say, though, that anyone interested in getting involved in the animal-rights movement can find one or more organizations in their area.

PETA, founded in Virginia by Ingrid Newkirk and Alex Pacheco in 1980, has been perhaps the most **vociferous** animal-rights group. Based in the U.S. and with offices in several other countries, PETA's overall mission includes eliminating the use of animals for laboratory testing, as well as for food, clothing, and entertainment.

PETA's first major victory in the battle against animal testing came in 1981. Its undercover investigation revealed inhumane treatment of 17 monkeys at a research facility in Silver Spring, Maryland, resulting in the first-ever police raid in the U.S. on an animal laboratory. It was also the first **confiscation** of abused laboratory animals, and the first U.S. Supreme Court decision in favor of animals in laboratories, according to PETA.

Animal supporters also protest against the use of animal fur.

Since then, PETA has participated in many similar victories. They helped create a permanent ban on shooting dogs and cats in U.S. military "wound laboratories" in 1983. Three years later, they ended the confinement of chimpanzees at a Maryland lab in 1986. In 1993, PETA led the fight that outlawed the worldwide end of using live pigs and ferrets in car-crash tests. After PETA objections, NASA dropped out of an international research program in which monkeys were strapped into straitjackets and launched into space. PETA also persuaded chemical companies and the EPA to drop plans for painful chemical tests on thousands of animals and convinced several beverage companies to stop all

PETA and other groups use marketing to spread the word.

CRUELTY *crueltyfree*
FREE WEEK!

ANIMAL
TESTING
FACTS!

animal testing. In 2014, the group formed the PETA International Science Consortium Ltd., which works with industry, private research facilities, and governments to promote non-animal tests globally. Around the world, PETA continues to work for an end to animal testing of all kinds.

Other Groups in the Fight

The Humane Society of the United States (HSUS) stops short of calling for a total ban of animal testing, instead advocating for the 3Rs strategy. But it has also successfully campaigned against abusive research. In its work to find alternatives, the HSUS has helped secure millions of dollars to develop new test methods in Europe, Brazil, and the U.S. In 2013, the global #BeCrueltyFree campaign helped persuade the European Union to ban the sale of cosmetic products and ingredients that were newly tested on animals.

The ASPCA today is one of the largest animal-rights organizations in the world, with local chapters across the U.S. and more than two million supporters. As part of its anti-cruelty mission, the group focuses on animal homelessness with adoption and rescue programs. Rather than advocating for a total ban on animal testing, the ASPCA states on its website that "animals should be used only when there are no alternatives and the research is likely to produce new and substantive information that will benefit human and animal health. Whenever possible, an effort should be made to find adoptive homes for animals used in experiments."

Founded in 1895, the Boston-based New England Anti-Vivisection Society (NEAVS) describes itself as a national animal-advocacy organization dedicated to ending the use of animals in research, testing, and science education. "Through research, outreach, education, legislation, and policy change," its website says, "NEAVS advocates for re-

BEAGLE FREEDOM BILL

In 2016, New York Governor Andrew Cuomo signed the Beagle Freedom Bill, which mandates that dogs and cats used in state-funded experiments have to be put up for adoption after the tests have ended. California, Connecticut, Minnesota, and Nevada have all passed similar laws.

placing animals with modern alternatives that are ethically, humanely, and scientifically superior."

NEAVS began as an opponent to animal research at Harvard University and the school's vivisection experiments. Over the years, it has combined that pursuit with other social movements. Like PETA, the HSUS, and other animal-rights groups, NEAVS funds investigations to expose inhumane animal research, labs, and companies and helps pass laws to protect animals. In 2003, NEAVS launched a major campaign called "Project R&R: Release and Restitution for Chimpanzees in U.S. Laboratories." The effort contributed to passage of the Great Ape Protection and Cost Savings Act, a federal bill to prohibit the use of chimpanzees in invasive research. The bill also released all federally owned chimpanzees into permanent sanctuary at centers such as Chimp Haven.

Victories Mount Up

No doubt, part of the reason that law passed was the growing public disapproval of animal testing. A Gallup poll found that 67 percent of Americans were "very concerned" or "somewhat concerned" about animals used in research. A Pew Research poll taken the same time found

50 percent of American adults opposed the use of animals in research.

Sanctuary chimps get new home

Animal-rights advocates declared a major victory in 2013 when the U.S. National Institutes of Health (NIH) announced it would retire the vast majority of its chimpanzees from research. In 2015, NIH announced that its remaining 50 research chimpanzees were to be retired to the Federal Chimpanzee Sanctuary System. That left the African nation of Gabon as the only country in the world that still experiments on chimpanzees. In perhaps the final roadblock to any future attempts to experiment on captive chimps in the U.S., in 2015 they were added to the Endangered Species Act, which would outlaw such testing.

In recent years, the animal-rights movement has claimed many other wins. At least 15 states now allow students to choose not to dissect animals. All but two states have banned pound seizures, the practice of state-run animal shelters sending homeless animals to facilities and universities for research or testing. In 2010, reacting to negative publicity, NASA dropped plans for radiation experiments on dozens of monkeys.

By the beginning of the 21st century, medical schools

had been gradually cutting back on their animal-testing programs. For years, dogs, cats, pigs, and other animals were used by med schools to teach students. They practiced applying anesthesia, removing organs, cutting incisions, finding a large vein, and performing other surgical procedures. After the lessons, the animals were routinely destroyed. Animals-rights groups had been advocating for the end of such experiments for decades. Since 1985, the Physicians Committee for Responsible Medicine, a group of 12,000 doctors, has been a voice in the fight.

All those efforts have paid off. In May 2016, Johns Hopkins University School of Medicine in Baltimore abandoned the use of live pigs in its student training, choosing to use

The movement to keep animals from med schools is growing.

Activists are hoping to make all animals safe from testing.

simulators. That left the University of Tennessee Health Science Center's College of Medicine in Chattanooga as the only medical school in the U.S. and Canada using live animals for student experiments. A few weeks later, the Tennessee med school announced that it, too, would stop animal testing. "With that decision, we entered the post-animal era in medical student education," said John Pippin, M.D., the school's interim dean. "Like every other medical school in the United States and Canada, the University of Tennessee acknowledged that simulation and other non-animal teaching methods have [taken the place of] the unnecessary use of live animals in physician training."

The long, and often controversial, history of animal testing has reached a tipping point. There's no doubt that many important human lifesaving or life-prolonging medical and drug discoveries have been made by testing procedures and substances on animals. Animal testing has also led to important advances in producing safer food, cosmetics, and household products. But progress in developing alternative testing methods, specifically ones that don't involve animals, have diluted the argument in favor of animal testing. As well, a majority of citizens have voiced their strong opposition to animal testing, based solely on moral and ethical grounds. For the good of planet Earth—all its species—the days of animal testing appear to be near an end.

 ## TEXT-DEPENDENT QUESTIONS

1. What kind of animals were confiscated in Maryland?
2. What does NE stand for in NEAVS?
3. What did Johns Hopkins do in 2016 that was such big news?

RESEARCH PROJECT

Pick one of the organizations listed here and research it. Put together a brochure or poster that encourages people to join the group, using information about their mission or their goals.

For hundreds of years, concerned citizens around the world have advocated for the end of animal testing. There have been many success stories, including the discovery of alternative methods and passage of laws banning animal cruelty and testing. But the struggle goes on, much of it with the energy and determination of individuals.

There are several ways that just about anyone can get involved in the effort. The HSUS, PETA, and NEAVS are among many animal rights organizations whose leaders, members, and volunteers actively campaign against animal testing. Their websites provide information on how to join, donate money, and participate in campaigns—everything from calling government officials to marching in the streets.

PETA invites people over age 22 to join their Action Team, which of-

fers information on animal rights issues and ways to participate in or organize protests. The HSUS "Take Action" page on its web-

site lists dozens of national and local campaigns, such as anti-trapping laws, protecting coyotes, and saving elephants from poaching. NEAVS also has a "Take Action" page, which suggests more than a dozen ways to get involved, including asking friends and families to shop cruelty-free

and urging high schools and colleges to stop animal dissection.

Other national and local groups, such as the ASPCA, oppose animal testing and inhumane treatment, but mostly focus on shelters and other types of safe havens for animals. Their websites also offer memberships, often to local chapters, and solicit donations.

An Internet search for "animal rights groups" will identify and link to many of these types of organizations. Charity Navigator and Charity Watch operate websites that list and rate animal-rights groups. Crowdfunding websites, such as GoFundMe.com, Kickstarter.com, Indiegogo.com, and LoveAnimals.org, help individuals and groups launch animal-rights campaigns and connect them to donors.

FIND OUT MORE

BOOKS

Cohen, Jon. *Almost Chimpanzee: Searching for What Makes Us Human, in Rainforests, Labs, Sanctuaries, and Zoos.* New York: Times Books, 2010.

Singer, Peter. *Animal Liberation.* New York: Harper Perennial, 2009 (originally published in 1975).

Williams, Erin and Marge DeMello. *Why Animals Matter: The Case for Animal Protection.* New York: Prometheus Books, 2009.

WEBSITES

www.peta.org
The website of the People for the Ethical Treatment of Animals

www.www.chimphaven.org
Find out how this sanctuary is helping protect chimps.

www.speakingofresearch.com
To understand another viewpoint, read articles on this site which supports limited animal testing.

🔑 SERIES GLOSSARY OF KEY TERMS

acidification the process of making something have a higher acid concentration, a process happening now to world oceans

activist someone who works for a particular cause or issue

biodiverse having a large variety of plants and animals in a particular area

ecosystem the places where many species live, and how they interact with each other and their environment

habitat the type of area a particular type of animal typically lives in, with a common landscape, climate, and food sources

keystone a part of a system that everything else depends on

poaching illegally killing protected or privately-owned animals

pollination the process of fertilizing plants, often accomplished by transferring pollen from plant to plant

sustain to keep up something over a long period of time

toxin a poison

INDEX

PHOTO CREDITS

ABOUT THE AUTHOR

Bob Woods is a writer based in Madison, Connecticut, where he peacefully coexists alongside a diverse population of animals that inhabit the state forest behind his family's house. His work has appeared in a wide range of magazines, books, and websites.